The Next Step for Communities:
Teaching Entrepreneurship

"LUNI" LIBES

LUNARMOBISCUIT PUBLISHING

Edited by Monica Aufrecht

Published by Lunarmobiscuit Publishing

PRINT ISBN 978-0-9980947-8-6

BEFORE YOU BEGIN

IS THIS BOOK FOR YOU?

THIS BOOK IS for anyone who is interested in growing entrepreneurship in their city, country, or region. There are thousands of programs around the world that try to help entrepreneurs, and this book aims to explain what works, what only looks like it works, and what doesn't help at all.

If you have no experience with such programs or no experience as an entrepreneur don't worry, I'll do my best to explain it all in plain English.

"TYPICALLY"

THIS BOOK IS going to make a lot of definitive statements. E.g., "first-time entrepreneurs need a lot of hands on guidance." It gets monotonous to include the word "typically" or "usually" in all those statements, so please add them in your mind. There are exceptions to every otherwise hard and fast rule.

THE NEXT STEP FOR COMMUNITIES

CONTENTS

THE NEXT STEP FOR COMMUNITIES

THE MINDSET

TRAITS OF AN ENTREPRENUR

CAN ENTREPRENEURSHIP BE TAUGHT?

FIRST AND FOREMOST let's start with the big, controversial question, "Can entrepreneurship be taught?" This is really a whole series of questions:

1. Is there something special about entrepreneurs?
2. If so, are they born that way, or can the entrepreneurial sprit be taught?
3. If so, what do they need to learn to be successful entrepreneurs?
4. If so, can that be taught?

I wouldn't be spending my time teaching entrepreneurs if I didn't think the answer to all of these questions is "yes." Yes, there is something different about entrepreneurs. Yes, some people are born with a personality that leads them to entrepreneurship, but yes that unique mindset can also be taught. Yes, there is in fact a curriculum that entrepreneurs need to master, and yes, that curriculum can be taught.

PROBLEMS WITH SOLUTIONS

Entrepreneurs are rare. In the United States, they comprise around 5% of the population. In the developing world, that percentage is higher, but far less than half the population. Thus everywhere entrepreneurs are the minority.

The key difference between entrepreneurs and the masses is the mindset that problems can and should be fixed, now, without waiting for others to act. An entrepreneur on his way to work, sitting in traffic thinks, "Is there no other more efficient way for all these people to get to work, either over or under all this traffic, or by having people work from home, or closer to home, or barring that solution, some way to make the commute more productive or more entertaining?" This is in contrast to the masses, who sitting in the same traffic either think, "Someone should do something to lessen this traffic" or more often "Traffic is terrible, but that's just the way the world works."

New inventions, new processes, new services all come about when entrepreneurs ignore the way the world works today and envision how the world should work tomorrow.

Some people are born looking at the world as fixable, but this is a mindset that can be taught. In fact, perhaps what the world needs to further human progress is to teach this mindset to every student in every school.

CREATIVE AND INVENTIVE

Entrepreneurs need to be creative and inventive. Problems don't provide their own solutions. If they did, the world wouldn't need entrepreneurs.

Creativity as an ability is another topic questioned like entrepreneurship. Are some people born creative or can it be taught? Given how much of elementary school time is spent having students write stories and poems, draw drawings, paint, and play music, it seems quite clear that educators think creativity can be taught. If not, then every test in every class would simply be multiple choice.

Entrepreneurs need to not just see what is broken or inefficient, but they need to invent solutions that other people will adopt. More often than not, they need to invent a few solutions, as the first often doesn't work as well as they expect. Often neither does the second.

RESOURCEFUL

Entrepreneurs need to resourceful. Few entrepreneurs have all the resources they need to create the solution they envision. They may need money to buy equipment and/or to advertise. They may need access to some talent that they don't have themselves, and can't afford to hire. Their needs most often exceed their means, but they can't let that get in the way.

Most people, when lacking something they need, give up and say it can't be done. Entrepreneurs either find a way to get what they need, or invent a substitute that works sufficiently well. Or in some cases entrepreneurs simply sell their vision as if it were real, and build the solution after the customers have paid.

That last path may sound like it borders on ethical, but Kickstarter has helped tens of thousands of entrepreneurs do exactly that, selling a vision to be delivered later, if and only if enough customers like the idea.

PERSISTANT

Entrepreneurs need to persistent. First and foremost because their friends and family usually call them crazy, tell them their idea won't work, tell them that if the problem they won't stop talking about had a solution, someone else would have solved it ages ago.

Entrepreneurs need to persistent because most of the people they think will be customers won't. The process of selling a solution is fraught with rejection.

Successful entrepreneurs do not give up when faced with lack of resources, unbelievers, and rejections by customers. They stay dogged in their belief in their solution, and find a way to make progress toward success.

OPTIMIST

Entrepreneurs are optimists. Entrepreneurs don't look at a dystopian future and call it OK. Neither do they don't look at the current world and say everything is OK. Entrepreneurs see a problem that needs fixing and envision a better world with a solution in place.

Furthermore, entrepreneurs will come across multiple hurdles and setbacks in their path to bring that solution to market. If they can not hold that better vision of the future in their minds as they look for paths over the hurdles and through the setbacks, their persistence will give out and they will give up.

GENERALISTS

Entrepreneurship isn't a specialty. Entrepreneurs need to be generalists, able to perform whatever task is next needed to move from problem to solution to paying customers.

The modern world doesn't celebrate generalists. Children are asked from a young age, "What are you going to be when you grow up?" Implied in that question is that you get to pick one and only one specialty. Academia forces college students to pick a specialty in the form of a major, and to study that one topic for two or three years as an undergraduates, then two more years for a Masters. Graduates are expected to pursue a focused career, learning and growing one set of expertise.

None of this prepares people to be entrepreneurs, where one day you are designing a product, the next day revising the financial model, the next updating a website, the next pitching to investors, selling to customers, talking to the press, managing the team, and so on, all while worrying about what happens tomorrow, next month, and next year.

A MINDSET

Combine a creative and inventive problem solver who is resourceful, persistent, optimistic, and jack-of-many-trades, and you have yourself an entrepreneur. A person with the so-called "entrepreneurial mindset."

All of those traits are teachable. Some may be more prevalent across society than others. Some may be actively suppressed within the populace by the rigors and rules of elementary, middle and high school, and thus simply need to be reawakened.

In any case, first and foremost when teaching entrepreneurship is to ensure the students have this entrepreneurial mindset.

MAPPING THEIR SKILLS

SUCCESSFUL ENTREPRENEURS NEED to be reasonable good at a wide variety of skills. They need to be generalists, not specialists, which is what the modern school system produces.

The reason entrepreneurs need to know multiple skills is simple: It takes a wide variety of skills to build a successful company. New companies do not have money to hire specialists to do all these varied tasks. New companies do not have the time to coordinate a team of specialists even if they could build that team. How can a founder (or co-founders) hire such a team if they themselves didn't understand how to do the various tasks. And most importantly, the founder(s) of the company need to quickly know when something is not working, and have or create a plan to fix it.

All that, plus the founder must be able to explain the company to potential investors and potential team members. To do that it helps tremendously to know the business plan inside and out. Building the whole plan is the best way to know all the details.

(AT LEAST) SEVEN SKILLS

Entrepreneurs need to be competent in at least seven key skills:
- Strategy & Tactics
- Design
- Marketing
- Sales
- Financials
- Fundraising
- Operations

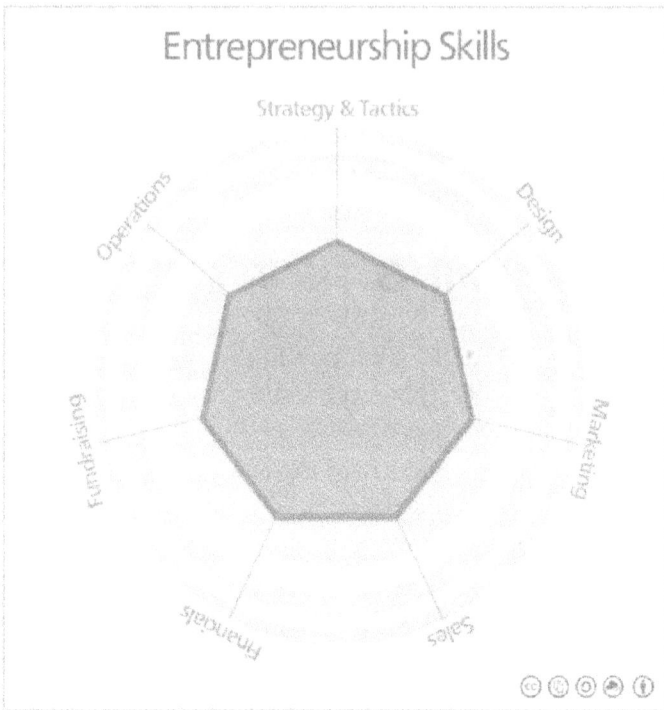

When I work with entrepreneurs, one of the first homework or due diligence assignments I give them is to fill out my *Entrepreneurship Skills Map* (see lunarmobiscuit.com/classroom/skills/). This self-assessment lets me quickly understand what to spend the most time teaching, and provides a reminder to the entrepreneur on what skills they should be pushing themselves to improve on.

Most first-time entrepreneurs' maps do not look like the above image. Most first-time entrepreneur have big gaps in their training and experience. The images below are what real entrepreneurs' skills look like in this mapping.

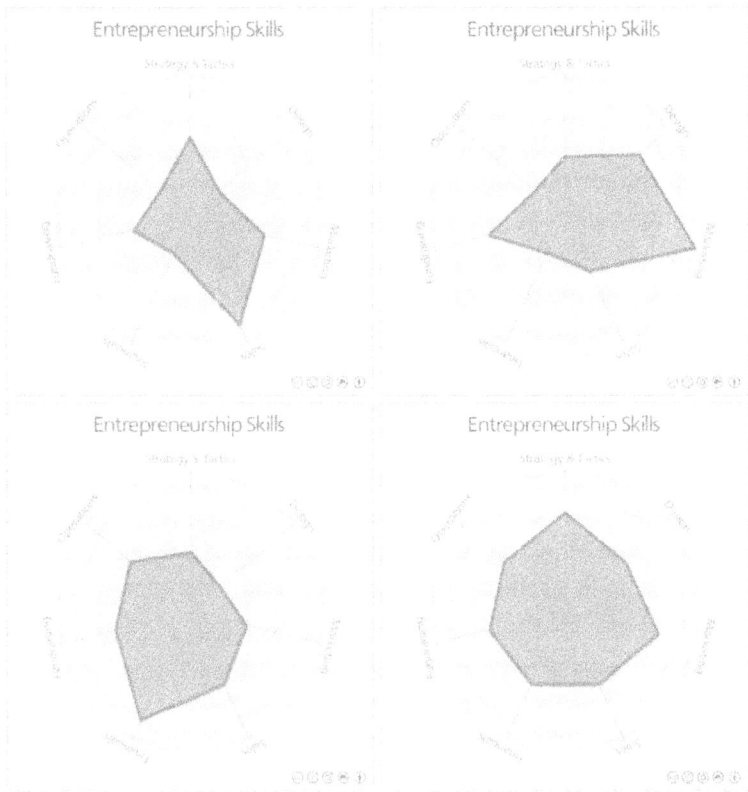

Entrepreneurship Skills

Entrepreneurship Skills

Entrepreneurship Skills

Entrepreneurship Skills

STRATEGY & TACTICS

The first skills is the ability to think strategically. To create a grand vision for what the company will be many years from now, and to devise a strategy to get it there.

Usually this vision includes a lot of customers, who will not share this vision when all they have to see is a new, small company. The path from idea to profitable company can be quite murky in the middle, like the gnomes' plan on South Park:

1. Collect underpants
2. ???
3. Profit

Filling in that missing middle step is where the strategy meets tactics. The plan not only needs a grand vision for the future, it needs the next few steps that lead to that vision. Those are the tactics.

DESIGN

This design skill includes the broadest definition of that term, comprising not only some ability in graphic design, but also the ability to design the processes and features within the solution. Design like the beloved user experience that Apple, Amazon, and In&Out Burger provide to their customers.

Here in the 21st Century, it is too easy to make a new company look like it has millions in funding. A professional, polished website that looks like it was created by a professional designer can be created in hours. Logos, business cards, and 1-pagers should all have that same level of detail.

Ideally the brand is well integrated into all of this, with the name having meaning or surrounded by the design elements to make it take on the desired meaning.

MARKETING

Marketing too is the broadest definition of that that term, comprising not only the ability to write the words for the website and 1-pager and sales brochure, but also to do the market research to understand the potential opportunity size, to understand the competition, and to explain all of that to others.

Once launched, startup marketing is about building awareness. These days that is often through social media, search engines, and content creation. In some markets it still means billboards and sandwich boards and flyers.

After launch, marketing flows back into design, understanding what customers want next, prioritizing those desires, and refining the road map to fit it into the living business plan.

SALES

Awareness is not enough. A successful company needs paying customers. The job of closing customers is the skill of sales.

Building a sales process is also part of this effort as is optimizing the sales funnel, qualifying leads, and dealing with the inevitable flood of rejection.

Sales also includes the skill of building a sales team, as most successful companies have more than one salesperson. Building an incentive structure for the sales people. Dividing the potential customers in a manageable manner. Managing not only the hunters but also the farmers to set up the company for repeat customers and long-term success.

FINANCIALS

Every new business needs some financial modeling. It's a waste of everyone's time and effort if there is no way for a company to ever be profitable or if the resources needed to reach profitability are beyond reach.

Finance also includes bookkeeping and accounting, keeping track of the cash-on-hand, the inventories, the assets and liabilities, ensuring that the company does not run out of money. No money, no company.

This skill also includes relations with investors, taking their money and ensuring it get paid back. Unhappy investors are an all-too-common pitfall that kills companies.

FUNDRAISING

Speaking of investors, it usually takes money to make money, and just about every company I work with expects that money to come from investors. This capital could be also be from a bank loan or a grant.

No matter the source, fundraising that capital is a skill. Do it wrong, and an entrepreneur wastes their time, frustrated as to why no one sees the value in their amazing, grand vision.

Investors expect specific facts, in a specific set of formats, with clear asks for capital using specialized jargon. Misspeak the jargon and investors will swiftly move on to the next potential investment.

OPERATIONS

Last but not least, the company needs to keep the products

flowing to customers or the service operating. It needs to pay the staff, pay the rent, and literally keep the lights on.

A lot of the entrepreneurs I meet are strong on the vision, and light on operations. Vision, design, and fundraising can lead to a well-funded company. Only operations can keep the company running long enough to reach profits.

GAP → FAILURE

A gap in any of these skills doesn't necessarily lead to failure, but it certainly increases the odds. Fail to create a viable strategy, and the vision stays a vision. Fail to design a compelling product, and no customers want to buy. Fail to understand the market, and the cost of acquiring a customer can exceed the price that customer is willing to pay. No sales, no customers, no revenue, no company. No money, game over. No operations, the lights go out and the entrepreneur needs to learn a new skill, how to shut down a company.

Many entrepreneurs, when pressed about the gaps in their knowledge will say that they'll hire someone on the team to fill it in. That is better than having the gap, but I'm dubious as to how often that strategy works.

Case in point, many entrepreneurs have no experience in sales. Most new companies have a lot more difficulty selling their product than they expect. So lets suppose an entrepreneur is great at everything but sales. They design what research says is a great product. They find an amazing name, launch a slick website, and get a ton of press coverage. They hire a salesman with two decades of experience in the market, with great references, who built a 100 person sales team at their last company. But sales don't follow. What went wrong?

It could be that the salesperson is doing something wrong. That this new product is too different from what they've sold before, and needs a different style sales process. How is the entrepreneur supposed to know if that is true, or if instead there is something missing in the product, or the price is too high, or the customers are simply not so worried about the problem that they care about this amazing, novel solution.

Unless the entrepreneur has been on sales calls before and knows what a successful call is supposed to look like, they can't tell whether the flaw is sales or one of the other parts of the business.

The same story can happen with design, if the product design is outsourced or built by a hired team member. It can happen in the marketing, with the sales people calling upon customers who have no awareness of the brand. There can be a flaw in the financial model, found only when the hired accountant starts producing financial reports that look nothing like the projected financials.

This need to fill in all of the gaps is why I believe most entrepreneur training programs are flawed. Any program that doesn't help entrepreneurs fill in these gaps is leaving their participants open to commonplace failures.

That said, entrepreneurship is best played as a team sport, not as solopreneurs, and thus what really matters is the gap across the whole founding team. This Skills Map can measure that too. Simply take each team member's map, make them each different color and semi-transparent, and overlay them on top of each other like so:

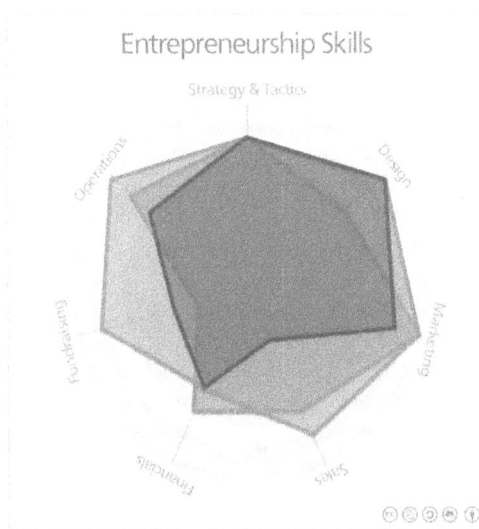

Entrepreneurship Skills

IT ALL HELPS

ALMOST ALL

FIRST DO NO HARM

LIKE A DOCTOR the first rule for helping entrepreneurs should be *first do no harm.*

It seems like any program that sets out to help entrepreneurs should be helpful, and thus it seems like there shouldn't be a way to harm entrepreneurs, but unfortunately that isn't true. There are plenty of ways to do harm.

WASTED TIME

The leading cause of failure for new companies is running out of money. This is more of a symptom than a disease, as the root cause to lack of money is in fact lack of customers. For a few companies, they run out of money before launching a product. No product, no customers, no revenues, no money, no company. After a product is launched, the list doesn't get much shorter. No customers, no revenues, no money, no company.

Anything that entrepreneurs do that isn't creating more paying customers is raising the chances that the company runs out of money. That finale may not come for months or years, but the one resources entrepreneurs can not make more of is time.

As you think about how you want to help entrepreneurs, first and foremost think about how much time you are asking of them. Think about the potential gain by the entrepreneurs divided by the number of hours you are asking of them. Be efficient with their time, as supplies are incredibly limited.

WASTED MONEY

Most new companies have only a tiny supply of cash. In the United States, less than 10% of all new companies receive funding from Angels or venture capitalists, and the United States has orders of magnitude more funding for early-stage companies than anywhere else in the world. Most new companies are started using the savings of their founder, his/her credit cards, and perhaps a little bit of money from friends and family. Money is thus nearly as precious as time.

Asking an entrepreneur for money should not be taken lightly. They are going to weigh the cost of any program against the likelihood that the program helps them raise money from investors or helps speed up revenues from customers. They are going to be overly optimistic in their assessment, as entrepreneurs are optimists.

Help them be realistic by only charging them money if there is no other way to provide the service or if the service is truly worth the price you are charging.

WRONG ADVICE

It is easy to provide advice to entrepreneurs. What is difficult is providing good advice that is likely correct. No two companies are the same. Markets change. New ideas are by definition untested. Thus even when a former entrepreneur is providing advice to a new entrepreneur, it is easy to explain what was done in the past, but impossible to explain what will happen in the future.

For some of the common hurdles that beset new companies, it is possible to explain the norms, expectations, and regulations. How to incorporate. How to file taxes. How to hire and fire employees are well known, highly regulated, and common to new companies and well-established companies alike.

Make it explicit when that type of advice is being given vs. an opinion. Anyone providing advice on the uncertain future should make it clear when he/she is explaining their own past experience or an educated guess on what may happen in the future.

New companies do not have time to make any big mistakes or too many small mistakes.

MARKING LOSERS

Contests are exciting. Winnowing down contestants to one big winner is done in professional sports, in beauty pageants, in the

Oscars and Grammy's and thousands of other entertaining contests. Companies are not created for entertaining investors or customers.

There are thousands of business plan competitions organized by universities and others around the world. I'll explain later the benefits of the model, but here I will point the big flaw. Business plan competitions create one winner, and then badge the other contestants as losers.

Anything that marks a company as a loser is not helping the company. That is one more hurdle for them to overcome, in addition to the time wasted participating in the contest, the money wasted on marketing material and travel, and the advice targeted toward winning the contest rather than in winning customers.

A similar dark mark appears every time an entrepreneurship program lists their finalists, then chooses a subset of finalists to receive something more.

If you want to help entrepreneurs, then tell the world only about those you are helping, and don't mention the others you've turned away. Let them quietly pursue the programs they think best, and only have to tout when they were chosen, never have to explain why some other company was chosen instead of them.

COASTING VS. ACCELERATING

Entrepreneurs make unbelievable progress when pushed and challenged. And they can spin their wheels and make no progress when coddled or left to fend for themselves.

Entrepreneurship training varies tremendously as to its length and intensity. I've personally taught a nine month class covering the same material as my ten week accelerator and six week pre-accelerator. The more that is expected of entrepreneurs, the more they accomplish. The harder they are pushed, the more progress they make in less time.

Many traditional economic development programs are six or nine or twelve months long. These programs generally provide office space and a monthly meeting with a coach. Many of these programs have no firm graduation event, no firm requirements for the end of the program other than a certain number of months elapsing on the calendar. They provide space for entrepreneurs to explore, but fail to provide an accelerant to get products into the market and to get companies selling to more and more customers. In short, they do far less for their companies than they could and should, wasting the potential of their entrepreneurs if only they pushed them harder.

PICKING THE WRONG COMPANIES

There are tens of thousands of programs in the world helping entrepreneurs, with hundreds more added each year, but still entrepreneurs are turned away by programs due to their own limited resources. For accelerators like mine, over 95% of applicants are turned away, even as we replicate the program into more and more cities.

The harm here is in picking the right companies to help. This is impossible to do perfectly, as no one can predict which companies are going to succeed. However, what we do know are which companies are most likely to fail. We know it takes a great team to create a successful company. We know team is more important than their idea, as a great team will listen to the market and adapt their solution to fit. We know it usually takes outside funding to grow, and we can predict which applicants are more likely to be liked by the funders.

Pick the wrong companies, and you not only waste their time, but you waste the limited resources that could have otherwise gone to another company.

The companies picked by the training programs need to be those that investors and other funders will fund after graduation, or those who can bootstrap with revenues from customers. Thus when picking for-profit companies, remember that investors' top priorities are team, team, and team. Don't fall in love with the solution, fall in love with the team and agree with them on the problem they are solving. Odds are their solution is going to change on its way to market.

EVERY LITTLE BIT HELPS

I HAVE BEEN A JUDGE in business plan competitions of all shapes and sizes. I've been a pitch coach more times than I can remember, and a mentor to more companies than I can keep track up. I've taught one hour, half day, and whole day workshops. I've taught six week, twenty week, and thirty week classes entitled "Entrepreneurship" for MBA students as well as independent entrepreneurs. For over five years I've operated a full-scale, intense, daily, ten-week accelerator program. In each and every case, the participants of the programs are grateful for the help. Every bit of help does feel good to them, at least at the time.

However, feeling good doesn't necessarily mean it is good. The big questions asked of the incubator and accelerator industry is whether any of the help truly helps in the long run.

From my personal experience I'd say unequivocally that nearly every bit of help does indeed help. But from watching all of these varied efforts, I'd also say that some of that help is more useful than others, and the amount of effort per immeasurable unit of help varies greatly from program to program.

For example, I've helped organize business plan competitions where hundreds of volunteers spend thousands of hours so that fourteen teams can present in front of a big crowd. I've been a judge at competitions that fly in four dozen teams from around the world, stick them in six rooms each with four pitch coaches, prepping for a final presentation in front of 100 or so supporters, to win a prize not much more than the cost of the travel, with no path for further introductions or funding.

Meanwhile, I've seen two hour workshops where fifty entrepreneurs learn one of the essential entrepreneurial skills, saving dozens of these entrepreneurs from repeating many of the most common mistakes, learning more in that two hours than from a whole complex competition.

I've also seen a few magical days at my accelerator, where one amazing mentor spends ten minutes sharing a bit of life experience that makes a world of difference for a handful of companies. And I've even seen a participant in my accelerator invent a new approach to look at financials and to share them with investors, opening new doors for all future entrepreneurs.

What strikes me in watching all this is the difference in efficiency. Going back to not wasting time, the question I worry about is not how to help entrepreneurs, but how to best help entrepreneurs using the least amount of time, effort, and money as possible.

That answer to that question is what drove me to write this book, so that others can use that question to most efficiently help their entrepreneurs, so that collectively we can help as many entrepreneurs as possible. They all need help and every bit of help does help.

ANECDOTES AND EXPERIENCES

MOST ENTREPRENEURSHIP TRAINING centers around sharing stories from other startup companies. Anecdotes. Experiences of other founders, often from the mouths of those founders.

This is nice, but tends to be more inspirational than educational, and may be one of the key factors that makes many people think that entrepreneurship can't be taught. Mathematics isn't taught by teaching the inner thoughts of great mathematicians. History isn't taught by listening to lectures of historic figures. Chemistry and the other sciences are not taught through a series of anecdotes about experiments. All these disciplines are instead taught through a logically crafted curriculum, analyzing the cumulative anecdotes and experiences into reproducible patterns.

Students are taught the patterns of mathematics, history, and science with a few amusing and interesting anecdotes added to make the class more interesting.

This is even more obvious when teaching English or any other language. Students are first and foremost taught spelling, vocabulary and grammar, the rules of the language. Only after those are mastered are the students expected to use the language.

NO BOOK

Back in 2011, I was asked by *The Bainbridge Graduate Institute* (BGI) to teach Entrepreneurship in their new Seattle-based "Metro" program. I had been a TA (teaching assistant) in the *Software Entrepreneurship* class at *The University of Washington* (UW) back in 2000, and I had hoped to someday teach again someday.

The class at UW was a series of guest lectures, by founders, early employees, and venture capitalists. It was a series of anecdotes and experiences. For BGI, I was aiming to do more. To do better.

I figured I could simply walk over my local library and grab a copy of *the* book on entrepreneurship, or barring finding one great book, a handful of good books. I came away finding no books at all. Thinking this must be a gap in my local librarians, I tried the *Seattle Public Library* catalog, only to find the same lack of books.

Undeterred, I went to *Amazon*, which back in 2011 had 4 million books in their catalog. A half hour later, I had a long list of books covering a wide variety of individual skills, ideas, and anecdotes: *The Art of the Start*, the *Lean Startup*, *Four Steps to the Epiphany*, *Crossing the Chasm*, *The Innovator's Dilemma*, but no book that explained the whole process of taking an idea and building a revenue-generating company. Or in other words, no book that walked a would-be entrepreneur step by step through the whole process of entrepreneurship.

Before giving up, I searched deeply at *Stanford*, *Wharton*, and other business schools to see what textbooks they use to teach the subject. Amazingly, their classes at the time were the same as the one I helped teach back in the end of the dot com bubble at UW. Guest lectures and anecdotes.

All this research led me to sit down and write the first of *The Next Step* series, outlining that missing step by step process for entrepreneurs. Over the next few years I further fleshed out the curriculum, adding books on marketing and sales, financial modeling, fundraising, pitching, and splitting equity amongst the founding team.

The books, along with a matching set of online video lectures forms the core curriculum when I teach entrepreneurship, whether it be to MBA candidates, within my *Fledge* accelerator, at open workshops, or wherever else I find myself teaching entrepreneurship.

I do include anecdotes and experiences from my own career, along with guest speakers and case studies, but they augment the designed curriculum, which ensures the students are taught the key lessons they need to learn to succeed.

FORMS OF HELP

BUSINESS PLAN COMPETITIONS

THE BUSINESS PLAN COMPETITION is a staple of universities, foundations, and others who use such programs to bring some excitement to their communities, at some expense to the participating entrepreneurs.

I have a strong bias against this form of help which I've touched on in previous chapters, which I'll explain in more detail here.

MISMATCHED GOALS

First and foremost, the goal of most business plan competitions is to showcase a winner (or two or three or five). The goal is rarely to provide training and guidance to the entrepreneurs, but instead to winnow down the participants in one or more steps to crown an ultimate winner.

Most often, these competitions focus on the pitch, presented in front of the judges, sometimes but not always with 1-page or other short business overviews to augment the 5-10 minute presentation. Most often any training centers around polishing the pitch, and occasionally polishing the written text as well.

The biggest problem is that there is a whole lot more to building a successful business than in crafting a compelling pitch. There is far more to business planning than can be summarized into a 1-pager or an executive summary.

ERRONEOUS JUDGING

Another problem is that the judges of these contests are choosing the winner(s) based on a short, exciting pitch. Based on the personality and presentation skills of the entrepreneur as much as the content. Those judges are rarely investing their own money in the winner, and thus have no incentive to pick the most likely business to succeed. Those judges are rarely spending more than a few minutes picking a winner, whereas it takes hours of due diligence to have any chance of determining whether any one company is likely to succeed.

Neither are these judges usually potential customers. Ultimately what creates successful companies is revenue from customers. If judges were asked to pick the product they are most likely to buy, they'd pick different companies. If their rubric makes them pick the product they think others are most likely to buy, they are doing so in markets they mostly don't know, and are thus unqualified to make that determination.

Meanwhile, as mentioned before, every participant who doesn't win is marked as a loser. Nearly every participant walks away being told they are not the best company, in a reality where best overall doesn't matter.

USELESS COMPARIONS

Unless two companies are solving the same problem, for the same type of customers, in the same part of the world, then these companies are not competing in the market. They can all find customers. They could all succeed. Which of them is "best" makes is irrelevant.

By this I don't mean that all participating companies have an equal chance of success. In every competition, workshop, class, and accelerator I've been part of, there is a spread of talent and difference in levels of experience. The odds of success depend on the actual competition in the market, the complexity of the solution, the complexity and duration of the sales process, etc.

Little of these factors are taken in account in most business plan competitions.

EXCEPTIONS

There are exceptions to this critique. One exception is the *Washington Angel Conference*, a copy of the *Oregon Angel Conference*. These are twelve week competitions whose primary purpose is to teach people how to be Angel investors, by having them screen actual startup companies within a business plan competition.

In the *Washington Angel Conference*, the judges are investors. They are putting their own money into a pool and collectively investing that capital into one company.

During the twelve weeks, they are doing a lot more than pitch coaching with these companies. They are digging deep into their business plans, often helping improve those plans through their questions and concerns. These are generally early-stage companies, typically in their first year of generating revenues from customers.

The prize is not insignificant to the participants, around $200,000. This money is what attracts the entrepreneurs to the program, as there is quite a large time commitment involved to participate through the whole twelve weeks (for the half dozen companies that make it that far).

Nonetheless, all of the companies participate anticipating that they will win the competition. Companies do not apply to first and foremost receive the guidance of the due diligence process.

And as much as I like this program, I have consoled quite a few participants who presented on the final stage, did an outstanding job at pitching, but felt like a complete loser after some other team went home with the big novelty check.

This program makes winners and losers, and those losers are talked about in the press almost as much as the winner, letting everyone in the community think they are flawed, with no note that they were one of the best six, by then all well diligenced and ready for funding.

A FIX?

Is there a fix to this fundamental flaw? Not that I know of. Contests bring excitement to entrepreneurial communities. The excitement and press coverage of winning can lead to investors and customers.

My advice is to start with any other entrepreneurship training first, rather than the shiny, exciting contest. That way you'll be able to see how much more useful and how much less work the other programs can be.

CO-WORKING SPACE

THE IDEA OF CO-WORKING is rather new, created in the late 00's and taking off in the 2010's. Today, in cities like Seattle, New York, London, and even Nairobi, there are dozens of co-working spaces to choose from. For startups, these are useful establishments, as they provide an affordable place to operate a business, some community support, and if nothing else, a place to feel like you are doing business, rather than always working at home or always mooching space in the neighborhood coffee shop.

In terms of startup training, they are at best places and communities where entrepreneurship programs can operate. The coworking itself is just a tiny baby step toward helping startups succeed. Startups need mentoring and education, and co-working spaces are great places to find such programs.

In my hometown, *Impact Hub Seattle* has been a great example of what a co-working space can do for entrepreneurs. My accelerator, *Fledge*, operates within the co-working space. We attract applicants from the community as well as applicants from across the global Impact Hub network.

The Hub is the central gathering place for social good, and thus nearly all of our mentors come visit us, making it efficient for those mentors to meet two or three companies in an hour or two, rather than having our companies scatter across the city to meet mentors.

Being in the middle of a co-working space means that any of the hundreds of people working there can turn into an unplanned mentor, and many do that, as they hear about the fledglings over lunch or join us in the morning status meeting. The same is true for people and delegations touring the space, as happens often, as Impact Hub Seattle is a popular destination.

The *Fledge Demo Day* takes place inside *Impact Hub Seattle*'s event space, drawing from the community as our audience and leveraging the awareness of *Impact Hub Seattle* as a key location in Seattle for inspirational events like ours.

Given all this, it shouldn't be surprising that I ran *Kick*, my pre-accelerator in the very same location. Most of my workshops are at the Hub as well, either in their event space, or upstairs at *Presidio Graduate School*.

Impact Hub Seattle is a bit special in terms of co-working spaces, as it has an accredited business school upstairs. For years I taught my MBA students in that building. That was a great commute on the days when *Fledge* or *Kick* was operating downstairs.

In short, having a central location where entrepreneurs, mentors, events and training programs can all take place is highly convenient for everyone. It makes helping entrepreneurs easier, which means it happens more often. But the space itself isn't doing the training, it is the place where that training takes place.

OFFICE HOURS

ONE LIGHTWEIGHT SET of programs found within co-working spaces are "Office Hours." This can be as simple as someone with experience offering to mentor anyone who signs up, for free, in 30 or 45 or 60 minute segments.

I've most commonly seen these Office Hours as a monthly recurring event. Meetings like these are part of the programming within a business accelerator, but in this case I'm talking about standalone mentoring outside of any other structured program.

It is not uncommon to see a few different people offer such Office Hours, each covering a different topic. It is also not at all uncommon to see these Office Hours disappear after two or three months, as the mentor gets busy with paid work, or after any month when no one signs up for mentoring.

There are three limiting factors to Office Hours which prevent them from being scheduled on a weekly basis.

First, it takes quite a bit of effort to find a place to meet entrepreneurs (even within a co-working space), to get the Office Hours posted on the co-working calendar, and to schedule time with each of the mentees. That can take as much time as is spent mentoring, and none of those logistics are as fun as mentoring.

Second, the odds of mentoring a company more than once are low. Startups change quickly. Monthly feedback to entrepreneurs is far less useful than weekly feedback, which is far less useful than daily feedback. In most cases the Office Hours are a once per startup, and thus less satisfying to mentors than when they get to see progress in their mentees.

Third, when nearly every meeting is with a new company, most of the meeting is spent learning about that company and its market, with little time spent on advice, opinions, and problem solving. When only 10% or so of the meetings include the fun part, the ratio of time spent mentoring vs. the time in logistics and backgrounds doesn't make sense for most mentors.

Fourth, there is no quick and simple way to filter mentees for quality. It gets frustrating an entrepreneur takes up 90% of the time talking about the problem space or market opportunity without ever getting to the issue that they need help with. That happens more often than you would expect. In those cases the entrepreneurs first and foremost need help understanding how to communicate succinctly, but by the time the mentor explains that, time is up and little else has been accomplished.

When *Impact Hub Seattle* was new, I scheduled some Office Hours, and experienced all of these issues. The same happened when I was an Entrepreneur in Residence at the *University of Washington*, helping their researchers turn their inventions into startup. I was paid a small stipend for that work, which perhaps made it even more frustrating when hours were wasted listening to "technologies in search of a problem."

Before I end this chapter, this is a fifth issue, but this time on the entrepreneurs. What I've learned mentoring at *TechStars* and operating *Fledge* is that five opinions from five mentors is far more than five times more valuable than one opinion from one mentor. For entrepreneurs, Office Hours doesn't provide a way to get multiple opinions. And first time entrepreneurs don't know the value of multiple opinions, and thus at think they have *the* answer from their Office Hours session rather than considering that they have just *one* answer and need to see out many more.

If there is a way to make Office Hours more valuable and efficient for both mentors and mentees, it needs to be organized more like networking rather than like school. Mentoring is ideally done en masse to entrepreneurs, with some follow-up conversations with whichever mentor(s)' opinion matched the final decision. That I've only seen done within an accelerator, organized as part of the accelerator, not the mentors.

WEEKEND HACKATHON

INTENSITY IS USEFUL for entrepreneurs, and a *Startup Weekend* or other weekend hackathon can be a useful tool to help entrepreneurs.

I think of these as opportunities to give entrepreneurs a kick in the pants. Often a kick (or strong shove) is needed to push a concept along between idea and reality. Often entrepreneurs get stuck, not knowing *the* next step (or *a* next step) in that process. Having a few hours with thoughts of a few volunteers and a few mentors can make a big difference.

For those volunteers, these events serve as a taste of entrepreneurship. For most people, the thought of quitting a job to start a company is a crazy thought (which it is), and the experience of turning an idea into a prototype over the course of three days is enough to persuade or defray that thought.

For those already stricken with the entrepreneurship disease, these events are a good place to receive feedback on their idea. Pitching the idea to a group and not having it gather a team can be a sobering experience, but one that can save that would-be entrepreneur a few years of effort pursuing a bad idea. Or that experience can lead to understanding how to better communicate that idea and in the value in preparing a pitch, both of which are needed out in the real world to succeed.

The short timeframe of these events attract mentors, giving entrepreneurs multiple opinions on their ideas. Plus the pace of the events are fast enough that mentors can see progress within a single day and share advice multiple times.

I've been a mentor at a *Startup Weekend* and a few other weekend programs, plus I helped create and operate two *#SocEnt Weekend* events back in 2012.

These events always feel good, both for attendees and mentors. Much of that is the intensity. Studies have shown that people bond who live through an intense experience, and 50 hours of work trying to turn an idea into a startup across three days is not an everyday experience.

Occasionally (but not as often as you'd think), a new startup company comes out of the weekend. Each *#SocEnt Weekend* launched one or two companies, a few of which later attended my *Fledge* accelerator.

While most of these weekends end with a pitch competition and a declared winner (or two or three), at *Startup Weekend* there are no cash prizes. There are thus no real winners and losers. Everyone who has fun is a winner.

That includes the organization operating the weekend. Except for them, there is one other calculation that matters, the time and effort spent organizing. It took a team of five more than 500 collective hours create, market, and operate *#SocEnt Weekend*. Ticket sales paid for the space, food, etc., with a surplus of money after all expenses. The team split those profits, but it was a tiny percentage of the 2012 minimum wage.

For *#SocEnt Weekend*, we were happy with that result, as we expected it to cost us money. It was, unbeknownst to the participants at the time, a *minimal viable product* for what became the *Fledge* accelerator later that year.

BUSINESS INCUBATOR

ANOTHER CLASSIC MODEL of startup assistance is the government-funded, industry-funded, or foundation-funded startup "incubator", where companies are invited in for 6, 9, 12, 24, or more months to build their budding businesses.

Most incubators include office space for the company, often provided for free or at a subsidized rate. Often a coach or two is also included, meeting with the team once per month. Sometimes these workspaces have lawyers and accountants, web designers, marketers, etc. in-house or on-call to help as needed, either for free or at a nominal rate.

I've talked to dozens of people operating programs like this in cities across the U.S., Europe, and into the developing world. They are so commonplace you'd think there was a study from the 1970s showing how government grants into such programs generate huge streams of taxes or 99% of all new jobs.

Personally, I've never heard of any well-known startup company originating from a program of this form.

From my experience with accelerators, these programs seem to be missing everything that makes accelerators so helpful. Mostly, the problem is the lack of intensity caused by the long timeline and the cadence of the monthly check-in. The one and only advantage startup companies have is speed, and the traditional business incubator plays against that advantage.

Nonetheless, a free desk can be a useful resource, one good coach is better than none, and sharing a space with other entrepreneurs can be helpful. Thus barring the resources to do create an full-scale accelerator, an incubator is a good place to start helping entrepreneurs.

BUSINESS ACCELERATOR

NOTHING BEATS A BUSINESS ACCELERATOR for helping entrepreneurs and their startup companies. If the accelerator is properly structured.

Do note that there are a lot of programs which call themselves an accelerator, which do not match the following description. The term *"accelerator"* has no clear definition and is adopted by some programs as it feels hipper and newer than *"incubator"*, which is it.

The modern business accelerator dates back to 2005 with the founding of *Y Combinator* and 2006 with the founding of *TechStars*. These two programs are not identical, but have much in common.

Fledge, my accelerator, was founded in 2012, modeled after TechStars, and thus is not surprisingly similar. However, I specifically made some changes which I believe to be improvements.

The basics of a great accelerator are:

INCLUSIVENESS

All startup companies are invited to apply, from anywhere in the world, for free, using an online application. Applicants are not specific to a single city or region or country, but open to the best entrepreneurs, from anywhere.

Some of the *TechStars* programs have a specific theme, and *Fledge* focuses on mission-driven for-profits, but that still results in hundreds of applicants.

EXCLUSIVE

The inclusiveness makes these programs exceedingly difficult to get into. They are all more competitive than applying to college at Harvard or Princeton or Stanford. This despite both *Y Combinator* and *TechStars* expanding more than tenfold since they started.

COHORTS / SESSIONS

Applications have a deadline and programs have a specific start and end date. Companies receiving (and accepting) and invitation all participate together within a single cohort.

Entrepreneurs are rare, and thus there are few times in the life of an entrepreneur when they are surrounded by fellow entrepreneurs. This alone is useful, made more so by the programming that nudges the entrepreneurs to help each other.

ONE PLACE

Participants all move to a single city for the duration of the session. At *TechStars* and *Fledge*, they work side-by-side every day. At *Y Combinator*, they meet weekly as a whole group and meet with the operations staff in between those meetings.

Having everyone in one place makes operating the program extremely efficient. It not only lets the staff keep up with the daily progress of the companies, it lets the mentors work with multiple companies on a single visit, and it lets the companies work together on common problems.

Having the companies away from their home cities or offices gets them to focus on the strategic thinking, mentor conversations, business planning, financial modeling, and customer discovery that they don't make enough time for back at home when trying to operate their company.

10-12 WEEKS

The sessions are short, just 10-12 weeks. Nothing is as powerful as a deadline. An unmovable deadline. It not only makes the entrepreneurs prioritize their work and eliminate the unimportant tasks, but also makes the whole pace of business speed up.

When an entrepreneur calls a potential customer or partner and says, "I'm here in *Seattle* for just six more weeks, participating in *Fledge*, and I'd like to talk to you about *XYZ*, can you meet this week?" the answer is more often yes than no. The people receiving such calls and email respond to the deadline too, plus as I've seen from teaching at a business school, they are far more open to helping students than other cold calls. Participants in an accelerator are treated like students in this context.

A FLOOD OF MENTORS

Many people enjoying helping startup companies. They enjoy it more when they can meet with multiple companies in a single day, in a single room, in an hour or two.

The short duration of the program attracts a flood of mentors. It prevents those busy professionals from procrastinating, from putting it off until next month.

Over fifty people come to help the *fledglings* at each session of *Fledge*. Fifty out of the network of over four hundred volunteers.

This is very similar in scale to *TechStars*, which calls this process a "flood of mentors." Each company meets with 10-25 mentors. That seems like a lot. It may sound like too many, but isn't. Meeting so many mentors is a magical process that helps entrepreneurs tremendously. It helps them find focus, find confidence, and often find novel ideas that lead to breakthroughs.

Meeting with a dozen mentors opens an entrepreneur's eyes to see the assumptions they have hiding in their plans. Some of which are wrong, leading to failure. Some which are correct but are nonetheless pointing the business in the wrong direction.

The end results of all these meetings isn't an answer on how to proceed. It is instead a new set of deeper questions that the entrepreneur didn't even know existed.

From this process comes a few potential outcomes. Sometimes, the plan is unchanged from where it started, but after these discussions, the entrepreneur can now explain why that is the right plan. Sometimes the plan is radically changed, pivoted, to something with a grander vision or something with a tighter focus. Most often it is in between, a far stronger plan with some minor changes, with Plan B, Plan C, and Plan D in tow from all those discussions, as Plan A rarely works out.

In all cases, when asked at the end of the program what was the most powerful part, just about every fledgling (and *TechStars* graduate) talks about all the mentors they met.

EDUCATION

At *Fledge*, we help fill in the knowledge gaps of our entrepreneurs by including *The Next Step* curriculum, taught in the first six weeks. This is one area where we differ from *TechStars* and *Y Combinator*. Both of them include weekly education in the form of guest speakers sharing anecdotes and experiences.

We do also invite guest speakers at *Fledge*, plus we bring our fledglings to visit other organizations to hear them share their experiences, but we spend hours ensuring our companies do not leave without some training in all the components of the *Entrepreneurship Skills Map*.

DEMO DAY

Y Combinator, *TechStars*, and *Fledge* all end with a *"Demo Day"* event. The name is anachronistic, but I've not seen a better name elsewhere and use it out of tradition.

The *Y Combinator* event has evolved into multiple days of pitches that are around two minutes each. No other accelerator copies that format. At *TechStars* and *Fledge*, *Demo Day* is an on-stage graduation-like event when the founders get to tell their stories to an audience of hundreds.

Format aside, *Demo Day* is the unmovable deadline. Participants know the date on Day 1 and plan accordingly. It is not an event participants want to miss the deadline drives results.

Demo Day is also a means to teach the entrepreneurs how to communicate what they do, why they do it, and why anyone should care. That itself is a useful skill, not only for fundraising, but also for recruiting and sales.

At *Fledge* we take this one step further, aiming for our entrepreneurs to give *TED*-like talks, rather than standard startup pitches. That is a far more challenging goal which takes far more effort to accomplish. We do not always reach that goal, but in the process manage to push our entrepreneurs to become far better and more confident public speakers, which is a slightly different, but also useful skill.

$20,000

Y Combinator and *TechStars* both use the same business model, paying their participants $20,000 per company. This seems counter-intuitive, especially given that they turn away 98% of applicants. It seems instead they should be charging far more than $20,000 per company to participate.

The reason the money flows to the company is that the $20,000 is structured as an investment. With that, the programs are not really 12 weeks in length. That is just the first stage of the program.

The founders of those programs were themselves entrepreneurs and as such, understood that it takes years to build a successful company. By investing in each of their participants, these accelerators (and *Fledge* following in their model) are setting up a long-term relationship between accelerator and company. They are creating an incentive for the accelerator to continue helping their graduates for years, as otherwise that $20,000 is nothing more than a grant, and these accelerators are themselves for-profit venture capital funds, aiming to make a profit for their investors.

INTENSITY

Add up all of the above components and you end up with an incredibly intense program. It starts with the 2% chance of receiving an invitation to participate, pushing applicants to do more, explain themselves more clearly, and to apply over and over again showing their persistence.

It then drops a bunch of entrepreneurs into a new city, for a dozen or so weeks, working every day to improve themselves. Add to that a dozen meetings with a dozen mentors, many of whom assign homework. Plus at *Fledge* homework from our class. Add a deadline for Demo Day, and the challenge of public speaking in front of a big crowd and video cameras.

College doesn't get anywhere near intense, not even in finals week. The closest in intensity to all this is *Startup Weekend*, but that lasts less than three days.

In the end, amazing work gets done in far less time than seems reasonable, and that time flies by in the blink of an eye. You are doing it right when it feels like two months passed in two days.

ACADEMIA

MANY COLLEGES AND UNIVERSITIES have classes in *"Entrepreneurship."* Some of these are in their "continuing education" programs (classes aimed at working professionals). I've taught such classes at *Bellevue College,* the largest community college in Washington State.

These continuing-ed classes tend to be quite short, only providing enough time for high-level overviews of the entrepreneurship process. My *Bellevue College* class was four hours long, all in one weekday evening. Four hours is not enough time to do more than provide a brief overview of the topics within the *Entrepreneurship Skills Map.*

This is incredibly short in comparison to the nine month long class in *"Social Entrepreneurship"* I teach at *Presidio Graduate School* to MBA candidates. I've been teaching six month and nine month versions of my *Social Entrepreneurship* class since 2012 at this business school *(BGI merged into PGS).* That is plenty of time to cover all the topics in depth, and enough time for the students to build a viable business plan or to discover a fatal flaw in their plan.

STICKING

From this experience, I would say that much of the myth that entrepreneurship can't be taught comes from academics working with students, or from investors meeting the students after graduation. The lessons taught in class are often not remembered by the students when they are working on fictitious business plans. Often the exercises are not practiced to the depth necessary to be remembered.

Or perhaps entrepreneurship is like every other subject taught in school, remembered for the semester only to fade away upon disuse. How many of us can still recite the capitals of every U.S. State, remember how to factor a quadratic equation, or conjugate *to walk* for a second person plural subject in the future tense in a Romance language we took back in High School and haven't used since?

IN-CLASS VS. THE REAL WORLD

What is most interesting is that I've been running the *Fledge* accelerator for almost as long as I've been teaching MBAs. As of writing this book, I've taught class eight times and completed eleven sessions of the accelerator. I use the same core curriculum in both programs, including identical books and identical recorded lectures.

I've specifically been observing the differences between teaching entrepreneurship to students vs. teaching to committed entrepreneurs. In more than a half dozen cases, I've had graduates of the MBA program attend *Fledge*, and thus that comparison in those cases is very much apples to apples.

Those students applied to *Fledge* knowing that they'd be receiving an identical curriculum. They wanted that refresher in addition to the mentorship. They wanted the rigor of the daily guidance vs. the cadence of weekly lessons in school.

INTENSITY

The difference may simply be that intensity. In addition to the six or nine month weekly class, I've also taught *Kick* twice as a six-week, twice-weekly pre-accelerator, again using the identical books and identical videos. Those entrepreneurs made at least as much progress as the MBA candidates did in six months, and again some of the *Kick* entrepreneurs were graduates of the MBA program.

One last bit of evidence comes from *FledgeX*, a 100% online, eight week variation of the *Fledge* program I ran as an experiment in 2015. A dozen entrepreneurs participated in that program, half Americans and Canadians, half African. We met them "face-to-face" on a web conference call twice per week, and worked with them one-on-one in between those sessions. Overall I'd say the results were much more like *Kick*. More learnings than class, but far less than from the true in-person, daily, 10-week program.

REQUIREMENTS FOR LEARNING

All this evidence points to intensity as the key aspect to teaching entrepreneurship. But that is not all that is needed. Entrepreneurship is a teachable topic given:

- Students who want to learn entrepreneurship
- Who have actual business plans to work on while learning the entrepreneurship skills
- Who have the time to devote to the breadth of lessons, undistracted by other classes or other jobs
- Who have their questions answers and who are provided feedback on their progress as quickly as possible (more than twice per week)
- Who have sounding boards and outside advice via mentors

That is long list of requirements, but take away any of them and the results I've personally seen look like class, *Kick*, or *FledgeX*.

Nonetheless, I wouldn't say classes are a waste of time. Compared to the other forms of training they are by far the simplest to organize. The least costly to operate. They can be online, bringing entrepreneurship training to every city on the planet.

My only warning is that they are more often than not insufficient unto themselves to guide a first-time entrepreneur through the whole process from having an idea to having an operational company.

FOCUS

LOCAL, REGIONAL, OR GLOBAL?

YOU'VE PICKED A FORMAT, have the team, space, and schedule all set. You are ready to get started. One big question before you start looking for entrepreneurs and funding is whether your program is local, regional, or global?

This is a question with no right or wrong answer.

LOCAL

Most entrepreneurship training is local to one city or one region. If that is your plan, you've got a lot of company. But before you think you are done with that decision, ask the question of what happens when an entrepreneur from a neighboring region applies? Or two regions over? Or from across the continent? Or a different continent!?

Entrepreneurs are hungry for knowledge and resourceful and many will ignore the boundaries you try putting in place. They don't care if your goal is economic development for your home city, as long as they get the help they are seeking.

Back when I was running *Kick*, each of the licensees ran in-person programs in a single city, with the license specifying their territory. The website listed those all those cities, and included a map. Meanwhile, entrepreneurs from all over the world filled out the contact form on the shared, global website, asking how to apply, and how to participate remotely. In a handful of cases entrepreneurs from overseas procured a visa and rented a room for six week to attend programs in San Francisco or Washington DC.

GLOBAL

Fledge, on the other hand, began with aspirations of being a global program. However, the first session included six companies based in Seattle and one company based in New York City, but with a founder I met in Seattle. The second session was all Americans, but with one ex-pat who was living in Singapore when he applied. By the fifth session the companies were from the U.S., China, Ethiopia and the Republic of Georgia, and that was the last session with more than two American invitees.

The reality is that entrepreneurship is a global phenomenon, and that thanks to the internet, and thanks to tools like Facebook, Twitter, Google, and Mailchimp, it is now possible for a training program in one city to make itself known to tens of thousands of entrepreneurs all over the world.

SPECIALIZATION

ONCE YOU'VE PICKED a territory, the other big question to decide is whether to also pick a specialization. Is your program open to any and all entrepreneurs, or just those working in technology, or clean energy, or agriculture. Is it focused on women entrepreneurs, or young entrepreneurs, or experienced professional dreaming of quitting their cubicle-based jobs?

The geography and specialization questions are connected. If you create a fine-tuned filter for the types of entrepreneurs there may not be enough of those entrepreneurs in any one city, or region, or country. At least not in a given six weeks or six months.

At *Fledge*, our focus is mission-driven for-profit companies. That focus eliminates 99% of the tech startups and 100% of the nonprofits. This still leaves a wide variety of companies, tens of thousands who are seeking training from a program like ours at any given time. But this focus is sufficiently narrow that can can't only serve one city or one region. We have to open applications to the entire world.

Programs like the *CleanTech Open*, which focuses on clean energy companies, solves this problem by organizing as a national collective of regional programs. A half dozen different organizations operate business plan competitions simultaneously, with the winner of each region advancing to a national competition. That adds a lot of complexity in exchange for the benefit of having people on the ground in multiple cities across a whole country.

APPENDIX

FURTHER READING

ONLINE CLASSES, MORE BOOKS, AND MORE ADVICE

lunarmobiscuit.com

MORE BOOKS IN THE NEXT STEP SERIES

The Next Step: *A Guide to Startup Sales and Marketing*
The Next Step: *A Guide to Building a Startup Financial Plan*
The Next Step: *A Guide to Pitching your Idea*
The Next Step: *The Realities of Funding a Startup*
The Next Step: *A Guide to Dividing Equity*

The Next Step for Investors: *Revenue-based Financing*

OTHER RECOMMENDED BOOKS

Startup Communities: Building an Entrepreneurial Ecosystem in Your City by Brad Feld

ACKNOWLEDGMENTS

THANK YOU TO Gifford Pinchot III, co-founder of the Bainbridge Graduate Institute (merged into Presidio Graduate School, *presidio.edu*), for his foresight into the future of entrepreneurship and his openness to my mind's wanderings.

Thank you to the team at Impact Hub Seattle (impacthubseattle.com), who have created a true community space that brings together hundreds of impactful entrepreneurs.

Thank you to the "fledglings" of Fledge, the conscious company accelerator (fledge.co), whose questions on entrepreneurship repeatedly demonstrate the complexity of turning ideas into startups.

ABOUT THE AUTHOR

MICHAEL "LUNI" LIBES is a twenty-plus-year serial entrepreneur, most recently founding Fledge, the conscious company accelerator. Fledge helps entrepreneurs who aim to do good for the world while simultaneously doing good business.

fledge.co *@FledgeLLC*

Luni is an Entrepreneur in Residence and Entrepreneurship Instructor at Presidio Graduate School, advisor to The Impact Hub Seattle, and to a dozen startup companies. He is also an Entrepreneur in Residence Emeritus for the University of Washington's CoMotion center for impact and innovation.

presidio.edu

comotion.uw.edu

thehubseattle.com

Luni began his career in software, founding and co-founding four startups and joining a fifth. These include: Ground Truth (mobile market research and analysis), Medio Systems (mobile search and advertising), Mforma (mobile gaming and applications), 2WAY (enterprise collaboration systems), and Nimble (pen computing, PDAs, and early smartphones).

This book, the whole *Next Step* series of book, Luni's online classes, and other writing can be found at lunarmobiscuit.com. *@Lunarmobiscuit.*

INDEX

www.ingramcontent.com/pod-product-compliance
Lightning Source LLC
Chambersburg PA
CBHW071639040426
42452CB00009B/1691